Smithsonian

THE SPOTSYLVANIA STUMP

What an Artifact Can Tell Us About the Civil War

by John Micklos Jr.

CAPSTONE PRESS
a capstone imprint

Capstone Captivate is published by Capstone Press,
an imprint of Capstone.
1710 Roe Crest Drive
North Mankato, Minnesota 56003
www.capstonepub.com

Library of Congress Cataloging-in-Publication Data is available on the Library of Congress website.

ISBN: 978-1-4966-9579-6 (library binding)
ISBN: 978-1-4966-9685-4 (paperback)
ISBN: 978-1-9771-5504-7 (ebook pdf)

Summary: The bloody Battle of Spotsylvania Court House took place in May 1864. The frantic fighting was among the fiercest single-day battles of the entire Civil War. How did the bullet-riddled stump of a once-mighty oak tree there become a symbol of the conflict? What can its story tell us about that day's battle and the broader history of the Civil War? Find the answers to these questions and discover what the Spotsylvania Stump can tell us about history.

Image Credits
Alamy: Niday Picture Library, 29; Bridgeman Images: National Geographic Image Collection, 45; iStockphoto: benoitb, 11, 32, 39, duncan1890, 12; LBJ Library photo by Robert Knudsen: 42; Library of Congress: cover (back), 5, 7, 8, 10, 16, 18, 19, 20, 22, 23, 26, 28, 31, 33, 34, 36; National Gallery of Art: Corcoran Collection, Museum Purchase, Gallery Fund, 14; North Wind Picture Archives: 4; Shutterstock: Everett Collection, 25, Morphart Creation, 13; Smithsonian Institution: National Museum of American History, 44, National Museum of American History / War Department, cover (bottom right), 1, 43, National Portrait Gallery, 37; Wikimedia: Muhranoff, 41; XNR Productions: 15, 21

Editorial Credits
Editor: Mandy Robbins; Designer: Tracy McCabe; Media Researcher: Svetlana Zhurkin; Production Specialist: Tori Abraham

Smithsonian Credits
Barbara Clark Smith, Museum Curator, Division of Political, National Museum of American History; Bethanee Bemis, Museum Specialist, Division of Political History, National Museum of American History

All internet sites appearing in back matter were available and accurate when this book was sent to press.

TABLE OF CONTENTS

Words in **bold** are in the glossary.

Chapter 1

WAITING FOR BATTLE

Confederate soldiers waited in their **trenches**. Rain poured down as dawn approached on May 12, 1864. The Confederate army was stationed just outside the oddly named town of Spotsylvania Court House, Virginia. They had one key goal: to keep the **Union** army from capturing Richmond, Virginia. The Confederate capital lay just 50 miles (80.5 kilometers) to the south. For the past three years, the Civil War (1861–1865) had raged. A Union victory here might bring defeat for the Confederacy. It would also mean the end for slavery in the South.

Enslaved people cutting sugarcane on a Southern plantation

Enslaved Black people did the difficult and unpaid work of planting, harvesting, and other tasks. Confederates were fighting to protect an economy based on the cruel practice of enslaving Black people and profiting from their labor. It was their way of life.

The line of Confederate troops stretched at least 1 mile (1.6 km). One part of the line bulged out in a horseshoe shape. The soldiers in this "mule shoe" were closest to the enemy. The Union attack would hit them first, and they sensed it would come soon. Some soldiers huddled under a large oak tree just behind the battle line.

The Civil War

In late 1860 and early 1861, 11 Southern states broke away from the United States. They formed the Confederate States of America. This government fought to keep the South's

The Battle of Chattanooga, 1863

system of enslaving Black Americans. The Northern states wanted to keep the Union together. This led to the Civil War. Fighting began in April 1861. It lasted until 1865. In the end, the Union won. The United States came back together. In 1865, the Thirteenth Amendment ended slavery in the nation.

Chapter 2
WITNESS TO HISTORY

The Confederate soldiers had prepared for battle. They chopped down many trees near the battle line. Then they cut the wood into planks and logs. They stacked this wood about chest high. These wooden defenses were called **breastworks**. The soldiers left openings in the rows of planks. This allowed them to shoot at the advancing Union soldiers. Of course, those soldiers would be shooting at them too.

One large oak tree stood just a few feet behind the Confederate battle line. Its trunk was 22 inches (56 centimeters) across. It probably stood more than 50 feet (15 meters) high. Why hadn't the soldiers cut it down? Perhaps they wanted the shade it would provide during the heat of battle. Perhaps the trunk was simply too thick to easily cut into logs for breastworks. In any case, the tree was about to witness a historic battle. It would later become a symbol of that battle.

Both Union and Confederate soldiers dug trenches and used trees, sand, and stones to build breastworks.

FACT!

Several types of oak trees grow in the United States. Most have wide-spreading branches. Oak trees can grow as tall as 100 feet (30 m). Some can live for several hundred years.

The Battle of Spotsylvania Court House centered on Neil McCoull's farm. McCoull grew corn and other grains on a farm of a few hundred acres. He lived in a modest wooden house. His three sisters lived with him. The farm's fields were dotted with trees. The large oak in question was just behind the "mule shoe" section of the battle line. It had stood there for more than 100 years. It would not stand for much longer.

The McCoull family farm

The McCoull family knew the Union and Confederate armies had been fighting nearby. A few weeks earlier, a battle had taken place in a thickly wooded area known as the Wilderness. The Wilderness was only about 12 miles (19.3 km) from their farm. The McCoulls may even have heard cannon fire on May 5 or 6. The two armies had also battled near their farm a year earlier. Then they went away. The McCoulls hoped the same thing would happen this time, so that their farm would not be damaged. That would not be the case.

FACT!
The McCoull House received heavy damage in the Battle of Spotsylvania Court House. The family repaired it. The house was destroyed by fire in 1921. Today, visitors see only an outline where the house once stood.

Neither side won the Battle of the Wilderness. Both suffered heavy **casualties**. But the fighting wasn't over. Next, the armies raced toward the village of Spotsylvania Court House. Several roads came together in the village. The army that controlled the village could move troops easily in any direction. If the Union army was in control, it would make it easier to advance toward Richmond. The Confederates had named that city as their capital.

The Confederates reached the village first. They quickly built defenses. Many of their troops were stationed on McCoull's farm. Meanwhile, the Union army gathered nearby. They prepared to attack.

The Battle of the Wilderness, 1864

The Union army marching to Spotsylvania Court House

Soon a frantic battle would overwhelm the peaceful farm. Thousands of soldiers on both sides would be killed. Thousands more would be wounded. The mighty oak tree that stood behind the Confederate lines would be a casualty too. Its fall would serve as a symbol of the horrors of the Civil War. This war split the nation for four long years.

But how had the nation become so divided? To understand that you need to understand the nation's long history with the horrid practice of slavery.

Chapter 3
A NATION DIVIDED

The Civil War began in 1861 after 11 Southern states broke away from the United States. The main issue was slavery. The nation had argued over slavery for many years. By the early 1800s, most Northern states did not allow the buying or selling of enslaved people. Many Northerners thought slavery was evil. They wanted to **abolish** it throughout the United States.

The Southern economy was built on slavery. Cotton and other crops grew on large **plantations** and smaller farms. The owners used enslaved Black people to plant and harvest these crops.

Enslaved workers picking cotton

Enslaved people were treated as property. Black families often were split apart and sold. Many enslavers abused enslaved people. About one in three Southern families owned slaves.

Not all Southerners supported slavery. Some realized slavery was wrong. Still, Southern states did not want to stop enslaving people. They didn't see how the Southern economy could run without it. And they said the U.S. government did not have the power to end slavery.

Centuries of Slavery

Enslaved captives are forced onto a ship for transport.

The first enslaved Black people were brought to Virginia in 1619. Over about 250 years, 12.5 million Africans were captured and enslaved. About 2 million of them did not survive the brutal journey to the Americas. About 388,000 Africans were forcibly taken to the American colonies, and later the United States. Many more Black people there were born into slavery. By 1860, nearly 4 million enslaved people lived in the United States. That was one of every eight people in the nation. Most of these enslaved people lived in Southern states. Nearly half of the people in Mississippi and South Carolina were enslaved. Some enslaved people lived in border states. These were states that allowed slavery but did not leave the Union.

The United States spent decades debating the issue of slavery. There was a balance in the **federal** Congress between Northern and Southern states. The Northern states opposed slavery. The Southern states supported it. In 1820, Missouri and Maine wanted to enter the Union as new states. Congress agreed to admit Missouri as a slave state. Maine entered as a free state. This action was known as the Missouri Compromise. It maintained an equal number of free states and slave states in Congress.

Representatives from the Northern and Southern states debate laws in Washington, D.C., in 1822.

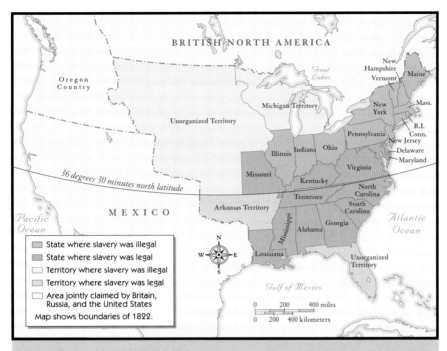

In 1822, the United States had an even number of slave and free states because of the Missouri Compromise.

Six more states entered the Union in the 1830s and 1840s. Three entered as free states. Three entered as slave states. The balance remained equal in Congress. None of these actions addressed the larger issue. The moral issue of slavery—the buying and selling of human beings—threatened to tear the nation apart. Southern states wanted slavery to continue. They wanted it to extend to new areas of the West. They even demanded that Northern states capture and return enslaved people who escaped to freedom there. Northern states wouldn't agree to this.

Tensions boiled over after the 1860 presidential election. Four candidates ran for president. Abraham Lincoln received about 40 percent of the popular vote. He won most of the large Northern states, though. This gave him enough **electoral votes** to win the election. Lincoln opposed slavery. He said slavery should not be allowed in places that were not yet states. Still, he promised not to interfere in states that already allowed slavery. He hoped this would keep Southern states from leaving the Union.

Abraham Lincoln

Despite Lincoln's promise, some Southerners feared the federal government would try to end slavery throughout the nation. Several Southern states left the United States. They banded together to create the Confederate States of America. Their government was based on supporting slavery. They chose Jefferson Davis as their president. Many Americans still hoped to avoid a full-scale war. Then on April 12, 1861, Confederates attacked a U.S. fort in South Carolina. Now there was no turning back. War had begun.

FACT!

Abraham Lincoln served as the U.S. president during the Civil War. He believed slavery was wrong. Lincoln once said, "Those who deny freedom to others deserve it not themselves." However, he wasn't sure the federal government had the power to end it.

Both the North and the South believed they would win the war quickly. Hundreds of thousands of young men volunteered to serve in the armies. They were sure that after one or two battles the other side would give up. But the war didn't end quickly. A series of bloody battles took place over four long years.

The United States side—nicknamed "the Union"—had certain advantages. The Union had more factories to produce weapons. It had more wealth. It also had larger armies and navies. The South didn't have many factories. It had to get ingredients for gunpowder from overseas. The North set up a **blockade** of Southern port cities. They hoped to keep the South from getting products from Europe.

Confederate soldiers, 1861

The Union Navy prevented ships from coming to and leaving Southern ports.

The South had some advantages too. Most of the battles were fought on Southern soil. Their armies knew the areas that would be easiest to defend. The South also had better **cavalry**. For a while, it was not clear which side would win.

FACT!

About 185,000 Black men served in the Union army during the war. About 20,000 served in the Union navy. At this time, the South struggled to keep enslaved people from escaping. Roughly half of the Black troops were former slaves from Southern states.

The Union capital was Washington, D.C. The Confederate capital was Richmond, Virginia. The two cities lay just over 100 miles (161 km) apart. Many battles took place in Virginia, as Union armies tried to capture Richmond. To the west, Union forces focused on gaining control of the Mississippi River. The river played an important role in moving troops and supplies across the South.

The war's first major battle happened on July 21, 1861. It took place in Manassas, Virginia. This village lay about 30 miles (48 km) southwest of Washington, D.C.

Union and Confederate forces fought in the First Battle of Bull Run in 1861.

Hundreds of people from the Union capital tagged along with the army to cheer them on. Some packed picnic lunches. They knew the Union side had the nobler cause and thought it would be a swift victory. Things did not go as planned. Confederate troops won. Union troops fled back to Washington. The spectators did too. This battle made one thing clear: winning the war would not be easy for either side.

Many major battles took place near the Union and Confederate capitals.

For two years, the tide of battle went back and forth. In the east, Confederate general Robert E. Lee stopped Union attempts to capture Richmond. The Union beat back Lee's invasion of Maryland. In the west, Union general Ulysses S. Grant captured two major forts on the Mississippi River. This was key to the Union's plan to control the river. The Union also blockaded many Southern ports. Still, as 1862 ended, no one knew who would win the war.

The Battle of Antietam, 1862

Union and Confederate soldiers alike felt the horrors of war. They marched through wind, rain, and mud. They fought battles at close range. They faced deadly rifle and cannon fire. About 620,000 soldiers died in battle or of disease. Hundreds of thousands more were wounded. Many lost limbs. Doctors had to cut them off to keep injured soldiers alive.

Freeing the Enslaved

President Abraham Lincoln issued the **Emancipation Proclamation** on January 1, 1863. This statement said that all enslaved people held in Southern states were now free. But the Union had no way to enforce this. And in a cruel twist, it did not free enslaved people in the Union's own border states. But it was meant to show that Lincoln still considered the Confederacy to be under his leadership. It also

The Emancipation Proclamation

pleased those who wanted to abolish slavery and kept England and France from supporting the South. Both countries made money trading with the South. But the people of these nations felt slavery was wrong. They chose not to help the Confederacy.

The summer of 1863 marked a turning point in the war. In the east, General Lee led his troops into Pennsylvania. He hoped to win a victory on Northern soil. He believed this might bring an end to the war. Lee's troops clashed with the Union army at the small town of Gettysburg. What began as a small fight grew into a raging battle that lasted from July 1 to July 3. Each day, the Confederates attacked. Each day, the Union lines held firm. Finally, the Confederates withdrew in defeat.

The Battle of Gettysburg was the bloodiest battle of the war. More than 51,000 soldiers were killed, wounded, or missing. Neither army planned a major battle at Gettysburg. But as more soldiers arrived from both armies, the battle grew larger. Gettysburg marked the last major Confederate advance into Northern territory. In November 1863, President Abraham Lincoln and others spoke at the dedication of the Gettysburg National Cemetery. Lincoln's brief remarks became one of history's most famous speeches. The speech is known as the Gettysburg Address.

President Lincoln giving the Gettysburg Address

The North also won a major victory on the western front. On July 4, General Grant captured Vicksburg, Mississippi. This city was a Confederate stronghold on the Mississippi River. Nearly 30,000 Confederate troops surrendered. The Union now controlled almost the entire river. This physically divided the Confederacy in half. Northerners cheered these two victories. They hoped the United States could soon win the war.

Then progress soon stalled. Union generals in the east gained no further ground after winning at Gettysburg. Both sides traded victories in battles in the west. By early 1864, Lincoln was growing concerned. The presidential election loomed in November. Many people in the North were tired of the war. Lincoln feared he would lose the election. He worried that a new president would **negotiate** an end to the war. Then the South might never rejoin the Union. In that case, slavery would continue in the Confederate states. Lincoln was determined not to let this happen.

Lincoln knew he needed to show progress toward winning the war. He needed a general who would take action. General Grant had proven he was a strong leader. He had won several key battles out west. He had captured Vicksburg. In March 1864, Lincoln gave Grant command of all Union armies. Grant soon came up with a new plan. He felt sure it would lead to victory.

General Ulysses S. Grant

Eight Key Battles of the Civil War

The Civil War featured dozens of major battles. These eight marked key points in the war.

	WINNER	
	CONFEDERACY	UNION
First Battle of Bull Run Manassas, Virginia, July 1861 The Confederates won. This battle showed that the war would not end quickly.	✔	
Battle of Shiloh Pittsburg Landing, Tennessee, April 1862 The Union won. The Confederates were forced to retreat after launching a strong attack.		✔
Battle of Antietam Sharpsburg, Maryland, Sept. 1862 Neither side gained any ground, but this battle was considered a Union victory. It stopped the Confederate invasion of Maryland.		✔
Battle of Gettysburg Gettysburg, Pennsylvania, July 1863 The Union won. The Confederate invasion of the North failed. Both armies suffered heavy losses. This was considered the deadliest battle of the Civil War.		✔
Capture of Vicksburg Vicksburg, Mississippi, May–July 1863 The Union won. The United States now controlled almost all of the Mississippi River.		✔
Battle of Chickamauga Chickamauga Creek, Georgia, Sept. 1863 Confederates won. The Union army was driven out of Georgia.	✔	
Battle of Atlanta Atlanta, Georgia, July 1864 Union won. This battle led to the capture of Atlanta in September.		✔
Battle of Appomattox Court House Appomattox Court House, Virginia, April 1865 The Union won. General Lee surrendered to General Grant.		✔

The Union had several armies. Up to this point, each had acted on its own. The Confederates had far fewer soldiers. They'd fought off the Union by moving their men around to meet each Union army. Grant wanted the Union armies to work together. He planned to invade Virginia with the largest group, the Army of the Potomac. He hoped to destroy Lee's army entirely. Meanwhile, another large Union force would try to capture Atlanta, Georgia. Atlanta was a major railroad center in the deep South. Smaller Union armies would attack in other places. The outnumbered Confederate army would not be able to defend so many places at once.

Brandy Station, Virginia, the headquarters for the Army of the Potomac, April 1864

Grant put his plan into action soon after taking command. In early May 1864, 120,000 Union troops crossed the Rapidan River in northern Virginia. Lee's army was waiting. A major battle loomed.

Grant's Overland Campaign

General Grant's invasion of Virginia in the spring of 1864 had two key goals. He wanted to wear down and crush General Lee's Confederate army. He also wanted to capture the Confederate capital of Richmond. The first battle took place in the Wilderness. It ended in a draw.

Grant kept pushing forward. "I propose to fight it out on this line if it takes all summer," he said. More bloody battles followed. By mid-June, the Union army reached Petersburg, Virginia. This was a key railroad center near Richmond. Lee's army was trapped. The end of the war was in sight.

The Union troops' positions near Petersburg

Chapter 4
FIERCE FIGHTING AND A FALLEN TREE

In early May, the two sides met in the thickly wooded area known as the Wilderness. Both wanted to gain control of a key road that ran through the woods. The smoke and many trees made it hard to even see the enemy. The weather was hot and dry for early May. In some places, sparks from cannon shells caused the woods to catch fire. Some wounded soldiers were trapped by the flames.

The battle raged for two days. Thousands of soldiers on each side were killed or wounded. Neither side could gain a clear advantage. On the third day, the fighting ended.

In the past, the Union army would have pulled back and regrouped after the battle. It might have been months until they fought again. This time was different. General Grant did not fall back. He moved the army toward Spotsylvania Court House. Several key roads met in this small town.

Soldiers battling in the Wilderness

FACT!

After one victory in 1862, General Ulysses S. Grant demanded "unconditional surrender" from the enemy. That meant he would only accept surrender on his terms. General "Unconditional Surrender" Grant became a nickname. It also played on his first and second initials.

The Confederates reached the village of Spotsylvania Court House first. They built a strong defensive line. Grant, meanwhile, prepared his troops to attack. Early on May 12, thousands of Union soldiers stormed out of the nearby woods. They charged through the early morning fog. The Union troops attacked the Confederate line at the bulge known as the "mule shoe." Many of the Confederates' rifles had gotten wet in the heavy rain overnight. They failed to fire. Union soldiers quickly broke through the defenses. They captured around 3,000 prisoners. The gap in the Confederate line was 0.5 mile (0.8 km) wide. A Union victory seemed certain.

General Grant riding into battle

The Battle of Spotsylvania Court House

The Confederates rushed more troops forward. This slowed down the Union advance. Fierce fighting raged all day. The enemy lines were often just a few feet from each other. Much of the fighting was done hand to hand. There was no time to reload rifles. Still, tens of thousands of bullets were fired that day. Many struck the oak tree just behind the Confederate line.

FACT!
The fighting on May 12 ranked among the deadliest single days of the entire war. The area where the fighting was fiercest earned the nickname "The Bloody Angle."

Darkness had brought a halt to many previous Civil War battles. But it didn't this time. Fighting continued after sunset. Rifle fire blasted through the night. Bullets thuded into the giant oak on the McCoull farm, caught in the crossfire. Sometime after midnight, soldiers heard a terrific cracking sound as the big tree fell. Thousands of bullets had struck it throughout the battle and torn away its branches. They had whittled down its trunk. Finally, the weakened tree could no longer support itself. Some soldiers were injured when it came crashing down.

A wooden plank on a bullet-ridden tree marks an area in the Wilderness that was destroyed by fighting.

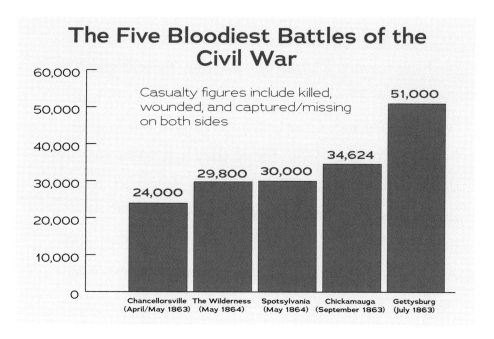

The Five Bloodiest Battles of the Civil War

Casualty figures include killed, wounded, and captured/missing on both sides

Battle	Casualties
Chancellorsville (April/May 1863)	24,000
The Wilderness (May 1864)	29,800
Spotsylvania (May 1864)	30,000
Chickamauga (September 1863)	34,624
Gettysburg (July 1863)	51,000

By morning, the Confederates had fallen back. But they built new battle lines. Thousands of dead soldiers from the previous day's fighting lay in front of these lines. So did the fallen oak tree. Several more battles followed over the next few days. Then Grant decided to move the Union army again. He wanted to find a better place to fight. The bloody Battle of Spotsylvania Court House ended in a draw.

> **FACT!**
> The oak tree, a piece of which became known as the Spotsylvania Stump, was not the only tree to fall in the battle. Other trees were also brought down by bullets. "We had not only shot down an army, but a forest," wrote an aide to General Grant.

After Spotsylvania Court House, Grant continued pushing toward Richmond. In June, he laid **siege** to Petersburg. This key city lay just 25 miles (40 km) from Richmond. Grant's troops fought battle after battle. Some they won. Some they lost. Win, lose, or draw, Grant kept pushing forward. Bit by bit, he wore down the Confederate army. Meanwhile, a Union army led by General William T. Sherman captured Atlanta on September 2, 1864. Then his army swept through other parts of Georgia and South Carolina.

General Sherman (center) commanding the attack on Atlanta

Lincoln was reelected president in November 1864, thanks in great part to the Union's many victories. U.S. voters saw that the end of the war was near. Richmond fell on April 3, 1865. Lee's army surrendered a week later. The Civil War was finally over. Union troops had achieved a historic victory for the cause of human freedom. The four-year struggle cost around 620,000 lives. It destroyed much of the land across Virginia. One casualty was the oak tree from the McCoull family farm at Spotsylvania Court House. At the time, not many people thought much about it. Over time though, its remaining stump would become famous.

Lincoln's Death

President Lincoln had hoped to heal the nation after the war ended. He did not get that chance. Less than a week after Lee surrendered, Lincoln was murdered. Confederate supporter

President Lincoln's funeral

John Wilkes Booth shot and killed Lincoln as the president watched a play. Lincoln had led the United States through one of its most difficult times. Union supporters throughout the nation mourned his death.

Chapter 5
THE STUMP FINDS A HOME

Long after the Battle of Spotsylvania Court House ended, memories remained. Confederate and Union soldiers alike recalled the fierce fighting. They remembered the bodies falling around the Bloody Angle. Some said they also heard or saw the giant tree fall. Many Union soldiers claimed their bullets helped bring the tree down. Thousands of bullets struck the tree that day. This means that most of the soldiers could have been telling the truth. They had no way of really knowing if their bullets struck the tree. It made a great story to say that they had.

After the war ended, Union soldiers began returning North. One soldier saw that the tree lay on the ground just behind the Confederate trenches. "The tree had been not more than 10 feet from the Union line," he wrote.

The battlefield in Spotsylvania Court House with trenches and stumps of fallen trees

Soon after that, a group of Union soldiers found that the stump was no longer there. They searched the field but couldn't find it. How could an entire tree stump simply disappear?

FACT?

Each year, thousands of tourists visit the battlefield at Spotsylvania Court House. Many walk the 7-mile (11.3 km) trail that crosses the battlefield. A marker shows where the Spotsylvania Stump once stood as a mighty oak.

The Union soldiers wanted to solve the mystery of the missing stump. They walked to a nearby inn. They asked the owner if he knew what had happened to the stump. He said he didn't. But a Black servant told the soldiers that it was in the smokehouse outside the inn. Moments later, the soldiers found it there. Perhaps the tavern owner thought the bullet-ridden stump would become a valuable souvenir. The soldiers probably saw it as an important piece of history. They proudly carried the stump to Washington, D.C.

In 1876, the United States held an event in Philadelphia, Pennsylvania, to mark the nation's 100th anniversary. The Spotsylvania Stump was on display. The Civil War had ended only 11 years earlier. The stump served as a powerful reminder of the war. In 1888, the stump was brought to the Smithsonian. Today, visitors can see it at the National Museum of American History in Washington, D.C.

The Spotsylvania Stump on display at the
National Museum of American History

FACT!

Nearly 10 million visitors came to Philadelphia for
the anniversary event in 1876. Many interesting
objects were on display. These included an early
telephone, typewriter, and calculator.

Chapter 6
A POWERFUL SYMBOL

About 620,000 Americans died during the Civil War. Spotsylvania Court House was one of the bloodiest battles. Roughly 30,000 soldiers were killed, wounded, or missing.

Once the Union won, slavery ended in 1865. But the fight for racial equality continued. After the Civil War, Black people still weren't treated as equal to white people. In many places, they had separate schools with fewer resources. Often they could not sit with white people on buses or in restaurants. They were even kept from voting. The Civil Rights movement of the 1960s helped to change this.

President Lyndon Johnson signs the Voting Rights Act of 1965 into law.

Spotsylvania Stump

Black people now have the right to vote and equal access to public places. While they have equal protection under the law, they don't always receive the same treatment. The nation still struggles to provide equal rights for African Americans.

The Spotsylvania Stump is still a powerful symbol 150 years after the Civil War ended. Like the nation, the oak tree bore the wounds of battle. It reminds us of the fight for a unified country and equal rights.

EXPLORE MORE

Abraham Lincoln's top hat

Lincoln's Top Hat

The National Museum of American History holds many interesting Civil War objects. One is the Spotsylvania Stump. Another is President Lincoln's top hat. Lincoln was tall and thin. He appeared even taller because he always wore a tall black hat. It became his signature fashion piece. Lincoln owned several top hats. The museum has the one he wore the night he was shot. It ranks among the museum's most treasured objects.

The 54th Massachusetts Regiment charges into battle.

Black Union Soldiers

Roughly 185,000 Black soldiers joined the Union army, and about 20,000 joined the Union navy. They made up about 10 percent of the total Union forces. Black soldiers served in their own units. They received lower pay than white soldiers. They also had white officers leading them. Often they were not allowed in combat. One famous African American unit was the 54th Massachusetts. The 1989 movie *Glory* tells the story of these brave soldiers.

GLOSSARY

abolish (uh-BOL-ish)—to put an end to something officially

blockade (blok-AYD)—a closing of an area to keep people or supplies from coming in or going out

breastwork (BREST-wurk)—a fortification built during a battle

casualty (KAZH-uhl-tee)—a person killed, wounded, or missing in a battle or in a war

cavalry (KA-vuhl-ree)—soldiers who travel and fight on horseback

Confederate (kuhn-FE-der-uht)—having to do with the Southern states during the Civil War

electoral vote (ee-lehk-TOHR-uhl VOTE)—a vote cast by the Electoral College, people chosen by the voters to elect the president

Emancipation Proclamation (ih-MAN-sih-pay-shuhn prah-cluh-MAY-shuhn)—a document signed by President Abraham Lincoln during the Civil War, which freed the slaves in areas under Confederate control

federal (FED-ur-uhl)—relating to the U.S. government

negotiate (nih-GOH-shee-ate)—talking to reach an agreement

plantation (plan-TAY-shuhn)—a large farm found in warm areas; before the Civil War, plantations in the South used slave labor

siege (SEEJ)—the surrounding of a castle or city to cut off supplies and then waiting for those inside to give up

trench (TRENCH)—a long, narrow ditch dug in the ground to serve as shelter from enemy fire or attack

Union (YOON-yuhn)—relating to the United States of America; also the Northern states that fought in the Civil War

READ MORE

Ablard, Michelle. *The Civil War: Brother Against Brother.* Huntington Beach, CA: Teacher Created Materials, 2017.

Herschbach, Elisabeth. *Black Soldiers in the Civil War.* Lake Elmo, MN: Focus Readers, 2020.

Schwartz, Heather. *Causes of the Civil War: A House Divided.* Huntington Beach, CA: Teacher Created Materials, 2017.

INTERNET SITES

The American Civil War for Kids
ducksters.com/history/civil_war.php

Kids in the Civil War
pbs.org/wgbh/americanexperience/features/grant-kids/

Social Studies for Kids: The American Civil War
socialstudiesforkids.com/subjects/civilwar.htm

INDEX